GW00645517

A Brief History of
English Catholicism

by
Fr Nicholas Schofield

*All booklets are published thanks to the
generous support of the members of the
Catholic Truth Society*

CATHOLIC TRUTH SOCIETY
PUBLISHERS TO THE HOLY SEE

Contents

ISBN 978 1 78469 005 2

Introduction

The history of Catholicism in England is largely hidden. Visit any Catholic church and you will find that (with a few exceptions) they were only built in the last two hundred years. Look at a list of diocesan bishops and it will go back no further than 1850. Get to know a local parish and most parishioners will trace their Catholicism either to a conversion (perhaps a few generations back) or a Catholic country overseas, whether it be Ireland, Poland, Nigeria or elsewhere. This gives the misleading impression that English Catholicism is only a recent phenomenon.

Look a little harder, however, and it is possible to uncover England's Catholic past, stretching back to at least the second century. On the back of any British coin, for example, you will see the letters 'F.D.' after the name of the monarch. This stands for 'Defender of the Faith', a title originally given by Pope Leo X in 1521 to the young Henry VIII when he wrote a treatise attacking Martin Luther. All over England the names of places, streets, even pubs provide evidence of long-forgotten Catholic connections – perhaps the existence of a nearby monastery or the cult of a saint.

This booklet attempts to present an overview of this hidden history. By its very nature, it will lack detail and overlook many important figures and events. Although Scotland, Wales and Ireland will come into the story, they will not be treated at any length since their ecclesiastical histories are significantly distinct and deserve a pamphlet of their own.

The danger with history is that it is very easy to know a lot of detail without seeing the broad sweep of the centuries - someone might be fascinated by Julius Caesar for example, but still have a limited knowledge of the world of antiquity. Many Catholics will likewise know about Becket, Campion or Newman but may feel unable to put them into the context of their times. This booklet aims to provide a general framework into which the reader can slot all the facts he or she already knows.

For the sake of convenience, the story is divided into four sections: (1) the long process of England's conversion to the Christian Faith; (2) the period of consolidation during the Middle Ages, when England was part of Catholic Christendom; (3) the Protestant Reformation which changed the course of English history; and finally (4) the "second spring" of more recent times.

Conversion: how England first received the Gospel

In 1604 the Jesuit controversialist Robert Persons wrote *A Treatise of Three Conversions of England from Paganism to Christian Religion*. The first of the conversions mentioned by Persons was thought to have occurred at the very beginning of the Church, when St Peter supposedly sent missionaries to the far-distant island. Then, in the second century, a British king called Lucius was believed to have asked Pope Eleutherius to send more missionaries from Rome. The third conversion was more historically certain: St Augustine's mission to Kent in 597. Fr Persons's point was to stress the Roman connection; England's evangelisation was largely due to papal initiative. The English Church was ancient and apostolic.

Persons's three conversions countered a rival tradition then being promoted by Protestant historians, which placed the emphasis away from Rome. Legend recounted how St Joseph of Arimathea had come to England as a merchant seeking tin (the West Country was one of the chief sources of tin in antiquity) and had brought with him the Christ child - meaning that the English Church actually pre-dated the Roman occupation. As William

St Augustine, first Archbishop of Canterbury, depicted preaching the message of Christianity from Rome before King Æthelberht on the Isle of Thanet.

Blake famously wrote:

> And did those feet in ancient time
> Walk upon England's mountains green?
> And was the Holy Lamb of God
> On England's pleasant pastures seen?

According to this story, St Joseph returned to England after the Ascension, bringing with him the Holy Grail, and founded the Church at Glastonbury. No wonder Britain was sometimes called *Primogenita Ecclesiae*, the first begotten of the Church.

The Romano-British Church

What are we to make of these colourful stories? How did the Faith first come to England? It is impossible to know for certain and, if the truth be told, the Gospel probably reached these shores in a more mundane way - through Christian officials, soldiers or merchants who settled in this remote Roman colony on the edge of the civilised world. There is no doubt that Christians existed in England from at least the second century, when Tertullian spoke of 'the haunts of the Britons - inaccessible to the Romans, but subjected to Christ."

Modern archaeology has uncovered evidence of this Romano-British Christianity - such as the mosaic of Christ found at Hinton St Mary in Dorset, now at the British Museum, which is one of the earliest portraits of Christ in existence. The early British Church was sufficiently well organised to send three bishops to a church council at Arles in 314, which sent its proceedings to Pope Sylvester. From the very beginning, British Christians were part of the Church Universal.

The first British Christians faced sporadic persecution, as is seen in the figure of St Alban, a citizen of Verulamium, the third largest town in Roman Britain near the site of the present-day St Albans. According to tradition, he hid a priest fleeing from the authorities and was so impressed by the fugitive's example that he requested baptism. When the soldiers came to search for the priest, St Alban put on his cloak and was arrested in his place. He was led out to the hill outside the town, where he was beheaded. Such was the scandal of his execution that the headsman's eyes are said to have fallen out at the moment of martyrdom. Devotion to St Alban quickly grew. St Germanus of Auxerre visited the martyr's shrine in 429 and helped spread the cult on the continent. Perhaps the most interesting thing about St Alban is that he may have suffered as early as 209, making him one of the earliest Western Christians that we know by name.

There were probably other British martyrs during the Roman period. St Bede tells us that SS Aaron and Justus were martyred around the same time as St Alban at the 'City of the Legions' (normally identified as Caerleon). Local tradition records that a thousand Christians were massacred near Lichfield - the name 'Lichfield' is popularly (if wrongly) supposed to mean 'Field of the Dead'. Likewise, St Augulus is sometimes listed as a 'bishop and martyr''. suffering at *Augusta* with eight companions (*Augusta* being a name given to London in the late fourth century).

Another famous early British Christian was St Patrick, the son, it seems, of a Roman official, who was carried off to Ireland as a slave and later returned to convert the heathens there. Less edifyingly, we might mention Pelagius, a Briton who travelled to Italy at the end of the fourth century and was responsible for one of the most influential of heresies: Pelagianism, the view that we can merit our own salvation through our own good actions, without depending on God's grace.

The Coming of the Saxons

Christianity seems to have taken a firm hold, although it was never total and it existed alongside the paganism of the majority. This state of affairs continued after the collapse of Roman Britain at the beginning of the fifth century. Parts of Britannia remained culturally Roman and Christianity was one of the most obvious signs of this continuity. However, the resulting power vacuum was filled by what historians traditionally called the *adventus saxonum*, the coming of the Saxons. St Bede described an orderly migration of Angles, Saxons and Jutes, each group setting up their own kingdoms. The reality, as suggested by archaeology, was less tidy. One recent historian states that:

> "the people coming together in fifth-century Britain were a real ethnic stew, hailing from across the whole of north-west Europe and, indeed, from elsewhere in Britain and Ireland."[1]

The Anglo-Saxon settlement was a long process and involved elements of invasion, migration and expansion from within, since Germanic and Belgic settlers had long been present on these shores. It seems that at one stage British rulers invited Germanic warriors, led by the likes of Hengist and Horsa, to help them fight the Picts and the Scots. Whatever the exact nature of events, the impact of these Anglo-Saxons was revolutionary. They came from a different world - pagan, illiterate and without such Roman niceties as coinage or towns - and it is little wonder that the British Christians became increasingly marginalised. Some managed to live alongside their new neighbours in relative harmony. Others were pushed out to the north and west, where Christianity still flourished, or even fled overseas - in particular to Brittany ('Lesser Britain') where many of the refugees are still venerated as saints. Some may have lost their lives - several martyrologies mention the shadowy St Vodine, Bishop of London, allegedly put to death by Hengist in 436.

Irish and Roman Monks

The British Church - or what remained of it - could still be remarkably cosmopolitan. St Patrick, for example, had been trained at Auxerre, and helped bring back to Ireland the idea of monasticism that he found there, which became such a distinctive feature of the Irish Church. The Irish monks were not just content to stay in their monasteries but were keen to make a *peregrinatio pro Dei amore*, a 'wandering for the love of God'. Along the way, they brought the Gospel to all they met. St Brendan is supposed to have sailed to North America - 'the Promised Land of the Saints' - in a tiny boat sometime in the sixth century. This is not entirely impossible - what are claimed as Christian inscriptions from this period have been found in West Virginia. Then there was St Columban, who set up monasteries in France and Italy. Many places in Italy, France and Germany still honour Irish monks and hermits who first brought the Faith to the region.

Another Irish success story, closer to home, was the monastery of Iona, off the coast of Western Scotland, founded by St Columba in 563. This became a true stronghold of the Faith, producing many saints and having a huge impact on the evangelisation of Scotland. In 635 St Aidan left Iona to establish a similar foundation on the 'Holy Island' of Lindisfarne, off the Northumbrian coast. This 'Celtic' style of Christianity thus became an important element in the Christianisation of northern England.

Meanwhile, in 597 (the year of St Columba's death) a group of Roman monks headed by St Augustine landed in Kent. They had been sent by St Gregory the Great who, according to tradition, first became aware of the English people in a slave market in Rome, shortly before his election as Pope. On seeing some fair-skinned boys he asked them where they came from. "We are Angles," they replied, to which Gregory responded, "Not Angle but Angels" and so, as St Bede wrote, "our nation hitherto enslaved to idols he made into a church".

St Augustine landed on the Isle of Thanet. King Æthelberht and his court met them in the open air, for fear of magic spells. The monks carried "a silver cross as their standard and the likeness of our Lord and Saviour painted on a board". As well as using these images, Frankish translators were employed to communicate in the English tongue.

Essential to the success of his mission was the presence of Æthelberht's Christian wife, Bertha, who may very well have requested the mission from Rome in the first place. The king had already given her the use of an old church in Canterbury (St Martin's) - evidence of the physical survival of the Romano-British Church - and she was served by her chaplain, the Frankish bishop Liuthard. During this period, Christian queens tended to have very important roles in converting their husbands to the Faith. The conversion of France is normally dated to the baptism of King Clovis (496), partly due to the influence of his Christian wife, St Clotilde. Christian women like Bertha were the "harbringers of Catholicism" in Western Europe.

And so King (later St) Æthelberht was baptised, followed by many of his followers; the sources say ten thousand. The faith of the king determined the faith of his kingdom. With the king's conversion came gifts of land. Canterbury was transformed into a Kentish version of Rome; the new cathedral was dedicated, like the Lateran, to the Saviour, while the nearby monastery was named after St Peter and St Paul. Relics were also sent over from Rome, those of St Sixtus replacing an earlier *cultus* to an obscure British saint of the same name.

The Legacy of St Augustine of Canterbury

In many ways, St Augustine's mission set the shape of the English Church. St Gregory's ideal was to establish two provinces each under an archbishop in the old Roman centres of London and York. In actual fact, St Augustine remained in Canterbury and founded bishoprics in London and Rochester, which were entrusted to his companions St Mellitus and St Justus. Another of his monks, St Paulinus, travelled northwards, baptised King Edwin of Northumbria (627) and became the first Bishop of York.

The conversion of the Anglo-Saxons did not happen overnight. Kings were baptised, others reverted back to paganism and there were frequent wars between them.

After St Edwin was killed in a battle against the pagan
Penda of Mercia in 633, St Paulinus was forced to flee
southwards. A year later there was a new Christian king
in Northumbria, St Oswald. The Church was quickly
consolidated, thanks largely to the efforts of St Aidan, a
monk from Iona who served as abbot and bishop from
Lindisfarne (Holy Island) - a reminder of the important role
played by the Irish in the story of England's conversion.
St Oswald himself also came to be killed in battle against
Penda in 642. He was venerated across Europe as a martyr;
even the little Bavarian church where the future Benedict
XVI was baptised in 1927 bore the Northumbrian king's
name. Although Penda himself remained pagan, he saw
the advantage of befriending Christians and even founded
a monastery in what is now Peterborough. Yet this was
not the last part of England to be Christianised. It was
not until 681 that St Wilfrid evangelised the kingdom of
Sussex and, four years later, the Isle of Wight.

It should be noted that, to further the process,
additional missionaries arrived. A Burgundian bishop, St
Felix, landed in England about 630 and set up his See at
'Domnoc' (probably Dunwich, Suffolk). Four years later
Pope Honorius sent St Birinus. Originally intending to
find "the most inland and remote regions of the English"
he found there was more than enough work to do in the
Thames Valley. He baptised the king of Wessex, Cynegils,
and established his cathedral at Dorchester-on-Thames.

The cosmopolitan nature of the Saxon Church is further demonstrated by an African and a Greek who arrived in Canterbury in 669 - St Adrian or Hadrian, a noted scholar who became Abbot of St Augustine's, and St Theodore of Tarsus, who was appointed Archbishop.

The mission of St Augustine established more visible links with the papacy, although it should be stressed that the Romano-British and Irish ('Celtic') Churches were part of the Church Universal presided over in charity by the Successor of St Peter. In St Bede's account of the 597 mission, it is the Pope who remains the central figure in the narrative, even though he never set foot on English soil; to this day, St Gregory rather than St Augustine is known as the 'Apostle of the English'.

Pilgrims began to make the arduous and difficult journey to Rome; the Northumbrian abbot St Benedict Biscop travelling no less than five times in the seventh century. In 688 Cædwalla abdicated as king of Wessex and journeyed to the Eternal City, where he was baptised on Holy Saturday by the Pope. He died shortly afterwards and was buried at St Peter's. In 726 it was the turn of the powerful Ine of Wessex who, according to tradition, founded a hospice for English pilgrims and instituted the 'Peter's Pence' collection, still made today.

It was also significant that St Augustine's mission was entrusted to monks, for the monastery or 'minster' became the chief instrument of evangelisation in England for the next three hundred years. These were served by monks or priests living the common life and typically served large geographical areas, until they were eventually superseded by the network of parishes that is still in use today.

The conversion of England, then, was a gradual process, largely due to three factors: missionaries sent by the Pope himself; Irish monks working in the north from their monastic strongholds; and survivals from the ancient British Church that dated back to at least the second century.

Consolidation: the medieval centuries

For later generations of Catholics the period following the conversion of England could easily be seen as a 'golden age'. England became the 'Dowry of Mary' and an 'island of saints'. There were great scholars like St Bede, a monk of Jarrow, who wrote the first *History* of the English People and helped introduce the idea of dating *Anno Domini* (AD). Zealous missionaries like St Boniface and St Willibrord effectively converted much of Germany in the eighth century, while at home pastoral leadership was provided by dedicated pastors like St Cuthbert of Lindisfarne or St Erconwald of London. There were powerful women, such as St Hilda, who ruled over a 'mixed' monastery of men and women at Whitby and hosted the Synod of Whitby (664), which met to reconcile differences between 'Roman' and 'Irish' Christians over such matters as the dating of Easter. It is interesting that well over half of the early English saints were blue-blooded; some writers have even referred to the system of government as 'hagiocracy', rule by saints.

The Vikings

Then the Vikings came. At first there were isolated raids, often directed against churches and monasteries - not so much because of religious hatred but because they

The West façade of Wells Cathedral, Somerset, England.

were easy targets full of treasures that could be easily carried away. In 793 Lindisfarne became one of the first victims, a catastrophe that had been suggested by famine, whirlwinds, lightning and (so it was said) fiery dragons in the sky. Described as "an undefended smorgasbord of ecclesiastical treasures, conveniently located in one of the greatest super-highways of the day, the North Sea", Holy Island was ravaged and many of the monks killed.[2] Writing from the Carolingian court, Alcuin of York commented that "never before has such terror appeared in Britain as we have now suffered from a pagan race." As G. K. Chesterton later put it:

> The world turned empty where they trod,
> They took the kindly cross of God
>   And cut it up for wood.

Other monasteries followed, including Iona and Jarrow, and the Danes provided hagiographers with many stories of Christian heroism. When Coldingham (Berwickshire) was attacked in 870, the Abbess, St Ebba, and her nuns cut their noses and lips with razors to repel the raiders and preserve their purity. Christian kings also fell victim, perhaps most famously St Edmund of East Anglia, tied to a tree and shot with arrows around 869.

What started out as raids eventually became, by the second half of the ninth century, full-scale invasion and settlement, with the Norse leaders attempting to incorporate the English kingdoms into their trade empire which reached as far as Constantinople and Newfoundland. Most of the north and the midlands soon fell under their influence - as can be detected in place names ending in *-by*, *-thorpe* or *-thwaite*. The great kingdoms of Northumbria and Mercia disappeared, and a long invisible line was drawn from the Thames to the Tees, marking off those regions which followed 'Danelaw'. Of the principal Saxon kingdoms, only Wessex remained and, under the enlightened rule of Alfred the Great, became the main centre of Anglo-Saxon resistance and the foundation (in time) of a united England.

Religious houses were left derelict and the succession of bishops disrupted, the Sees of Dunwich, Hexham, Lindisfarne and Whithorn disappearing from the ecclesiastical map completely. As late as 1012 the Archbishop of Canterbury, St Ælfheah (Alphege), was taken hostage by the Danes and killed in Greenwich. However, the Vikings soon settled down and were Christianised - an evangelisation from within, caused by their rubbing shoulders with Christian neighbours. This allowed the Church slowly to be reformed in the tenth century, during the reign of Edgar, thanks to the leadership of St Dunstan of Canterbury, St Æthelwold of Winchester and St Oswald of Worcester. Clerical discipline was tightened and religious communities were encouraged to adopt the Rule of St Benedict, inspired by the example of continental monasteries such as Cluny and Fleury. The reform demanded a firm resolve. At the Old Minster of Winchester, for example, St Æthelwold appeared at the end of Mass on the First Sunday of Lent 964 and offered the secular canons (who, we are told, were "given over to pride, arrogance and self-indulgence") the choice between adopting the Rule or the surrender of their stalls. By the end of the tenth century there were nearly forty new monastic foundations in England, following the *Regularis Concordia*, an English adaptation of St Benedict's Rule promulgated at the Council of Winchester in the early 970s. This not only provided universal regulations for the whole kingdom but set the monarch at the very centre, as patron, protector and overseer of monasticism. It should be noted that the period also saw the building of churches and the erection of parishes, which began to replace the older 'minsters' as local centres of faith and worship.

The Normans

1066 is still remembered as an epoch-making date in English history, when Duke William of Normandy defeated Harold II, the last of the Anglo-Saxon kings, at Hastings and ushered in a new regime. It was not a complete novelty - St Edward the Confessor himself had been half-Norman and there were already Normans on the episcopal bench, such as Robert of Jumièges (appointed to London and then Canterbury).

The Normans are often remembered as builders; many of their structures have survived the subsequent millennium, the churches as much a symbol of their power as the castles. William himself arrived in Sussex with a papal banner. Not only did the Pope judge the Duke's claims to be justified but hoped that the English Church might be reformed - in particular the scandalous conduct of Archbishop Stigand, who uncanonically held the two richest sees: Canterbury and Winchester. Four years after Hastings William was uniquely crowned a second time in Winchester, this time by a papal legate. William's seeming piety hid the fact that the Normans were essentially 'Frenchified Vikings' who just a few generations previously had been raiding churches and murdering monks.

William may have gained papal approval but he was just as keen to exercise control over the Church. It was, after all, a major force in society and the owner of land amounting to about a fifth of England. Moreover, churchmen had featured in the initial resistance to the Norman conquerors. By 1070 most of the bishops were Norman appointments, with the exception of St Wulfstan of Worcester and Siward of Rochester. The most prominent was Lanfranc, the new Archbishop of Canterbury, originally from Pavia, who had founded the great monastery at Bec and was a keen reformer. The episcopal map of England was redrawn, cathedrals in some cases being moved from their historic seats to more prominent towns - for example, Dorchester was supplanted by Lincoln.

Church and Crown

A theme that can be found across the Middle Ages is the constant conflict between King and Church. This battle was distinct from more recent struggles between Church and State, which were in part an attack on the Faith. All medieval rulers were Christian, with varying levels of personal piety but, as the historian Christopher Dawson noted, there was a battle between "the ideal of a theocratic empire and that of a theocratic church, each of which was inspired by the same vision of an all-embracing Christian society."[3] While secular rulers were keen to assert their authority and keep the Church in check, not only appointing bishops but investing them with their crozier and ring, the papacy promoted the pre-eminence of the spiritual power. St Gregory VII ('Hildebrand') proclaimed that the Pope alone could appoint or remove bishops and that he was owed homage from the Holy Roman Emperor himself. At the same time, the system of canon law was developed and more and more appeals were sent to Rome.

There were some notable battles in the resulting 'Investiture Controversy'. The second Norman king, William Rufus, did not show the religiosity of many of his line and had a tendency to keep bishoprics and abbacies vacant for as long as possible, so that the Crown could enjoy their revenue and lands. It took him four years to appoint St Anselm (a monk of Bec and now a Doctor of the Church) to succeed Lanfranc at Canterbury but before long the Archbishop found himself defending the rights of the Church and went into exile, only to return under Henry I. This monarch had marginally better relations with the Church, creating Ely and Carlisle as dioceses (the last to be made until the Reformation) and founding Reading Abbey. However the 'Investiture Controversy' continued and St Anselm found himself in exile once again. Eventually an uneasy compromise was arranged: the king would no longer nominate bishops or invest them with their symbols of office, but he would receive homage from them for the 'regalia', the lands and rights they held from the Crown.

The most famous English victim of this tussle between Church and State was St Thomas Becket. The son of a London merchant, born on the same street as another famous martyr called Thomas (St Thomas More), Becket served as Chancellor to Henry II and, at first, lived a worldly life. His appointment as Archbishop of Canterbury in 1162 led to a 'road to Damascus'-style conversion - he began to wear a hair shirt and, rather than being a docile puppet of the king, zealously defended the rights of the Church.

A particular cause of contention was the exemption clergy claimed from ordinary courts of law. This 'benefit of clergy' was threatened by Henry's *Constitutions of Clarendon* (1164) and led to Becket's humiliating trial at

Northampton and escape to France. He only returned six years later, partly because of the coronation of Henry's son as 'the Young King', to assist (at least nominally) in ruling the Angevin Empire. Coronations were the prerogative of the Archbishop of Canterbury and St Thomas quickly excommunicated his episcopal confrères of York, London and Salisbury, who had crowned the 'Young King' themselves. The result was Henry's famous utterance at Christmas 1170: "What miserable drones and traitors have I nurtured and promoted in my household who let their lord be treated with such shameful contempt by a low-born clerk!" Four knights made the journey to Canterbury and killed the Archbishop in his own Cathedral on 29th December.

The murder shocked the whole of Christendom. Henry and his French fiefs were placed under interdict; Becket's murderers were excommunicated and devotees began to make their way to Canterbury. The Pope swiftly canonised Becket - at Segni on Ash Wednesday 1173 - and Henry himself made a barefoot penitential pilgrimage to his tomb. Canterbury became one of the chief shrines of Europe until the Reformation. Many cures were claimed at St Thomas's shrine and pilgrims often took away with them a small ampulla, filled with 'holy water' from a well in which the saint's body had been washed. In the long struggle with the king, the Church seemed momentarily triumphant, although Henry still exercised as much control over ecclesiastical affairs as possible. In 1173, for example, he famously told the monks of Winchester: "I order you to hold a free election, but nevertheless, I forbid you to elect anyone except Richard my clerk, the archdeacon of Poitiers."

The struggles continued. When Henry II's youngest son, King John, refused to recognise the papal appointment of Stephen Langton as Archbishop of Canterbury in 1208, Innocent III placed the whole kingdom under interdict for five long years. This was a serious disciplinary matter, withdrawing sacramental and liturgical comforts from the people, with the exception of baptism and extreme unction. There were (at least technically) no public Masses, no church weddings, no burials in consecrated ground. The king at first remained calm, retaliating by seizing church property, but with rising tensions among the nobility and the threat of deposition, he decided to seek reconciliation. In a dramatic move, he surrendered England and Ireland to the Pope as a fief, only holding them as a vassal in return for an annual payment. This was a step taken by other rulers and suited both parties - the Pope won a victory in the struggle with the secular powers while the king had the Pope's support, which would prove useful when John sought condemnation of the *Magna Carta*.

Monasteries, Crusades, Church Life

The Middle Ages saw the foundation of many monasteries up and down the country, the royal and noble patrons benefitting from the prayers offered for them in life and in death and the kudos that their foundation provided. Establishing a religious house was also a convenient way of dealing with land that was disputed. New orders appeared on the scene, including the Cistercians, with their majestic abbeys at Rievaulx, Fountains and elsewhere. There were smaller religious communities as well, including the one home-grown order of the period: the Gilbertines, founded by St Gilbert of Sempringham in the twelfth century for nuns, canons and lay brothers and sisters. From the thirteenth century, communities of friars appeared on the scene, often building their houses in the middle of towns and working among the laity preaching and hearing confessions. There were several varieties, including the Black Friars (Dominicans), Grey Friars (Franciscans), White Friars (Carmelites), Red Friars (Trinitarians) and Austin Friars (Augustinians). With the foundation of Universities at Oxford and Cambridge, which were very much ecclesiastical institutions, the friars made a major contribution to scholarship and teaching.

England, along with the rest of Christendom, was actively involved in various crusading expeditions called by the Pope to protect Christians in the East and defend the Holy Places. Most famous among English crusaders was Richard I 'the Lion Heart', who played a key role in recapturing Acre (1191) and thus prolonging the existence of the Crusader Kingdoms. Crusading was often marred by personal greed and bloodshed but the aim was the good of the Church and the crusader's own salvation. As a result, even the saints got involved, such as St Richard of Chichester, who died in Dover in 1253 while preaching one such crusade.

Throughout the period England was Catholic and dissent was almost nil, with the exception of movements such as the Lollards, who (amongst other things) denied transubstantiation and preached a radical poverty. The Church was the dominant force in society. In the words of Hilaire Belloc, medieval Catholicism was "the soul, the vital principle, the continuity of Europe." The most obvious symbol of this was the local parish church, which could be found at the heart of each community, and was normally the largest, most imposing and best-constructed building, serving not only as a place of worship but also a town hall, a court of law, a theatre, even a marketplace. The church was not simply a functional edifice but, with the light streaming through the stained glass windows, carefully worked out geometric proportions and a wealth of images, it became a symbol of heaven and the hierarchy and harmony that were at the root of reality.

It was a dazzling world. If we travelled back in time, we would be amazed by the vibrancy of these churches, now long-since white-washed, and the drama of many of the celebrations. The West Front of Wells Cathedral (Somerset) is a good example. Impressive as it is today, it must have been doubly so when the five hundred or so niches were filled with painted statues. For solemn processions choristers stood in hidden singing galleries within the thickness of the walls - it must have truly seemed that the angels and saints were singing.

The Church by the early 1500s was in relatively good shape beyond the scars left behind by sinners in any period of history. There was a boom in vocations to the priesthood. Many churches had been rebuilt or extended. One foreign visitor remarked that the citizens of London "attend Mass every day, and say many Paternosters in public (the women carrying long rosaries in their hands), and any who can read taking the Office of Our Lady."

The monasteries remained not only centres of prayer and scholarship but social and medical care and agriculture. The Cistercian abbey at Rievaulx (Yorkshire) had a huge sheep farm and a nascent iron industry - at the eve of the Dissolution, advances were made there in developing a blast furnace, predating the Industrial Revolution by some two centuries. Many parishes had highly active and well-supported organisations called guilds, which took on a variety of roles - prayer group, charity, social club, trade union, local government agency and bank. Efforts were being made by bishops and priests to improve the catechesis of their congregations. Most of the first printed books were religious; not just heavy, academic tomes but works in English, such as the popular *Golden Legend*, containing the stories of the saints.

Forty Martyrs of England and Wales.

Crisis: the splintering of Christendom

Thousands of books have been written about the 'Protestant Reformation' and there is no room here to deal with it in great detail. Suffice to say that its impact was revolutionary - splitting Christendom into 'Catholic' and 'Protestant' camps, which were as often connected to politics as to personal faith. It shows that things had not changed since the time of St Æthelberht of Kent a thousand years before. Religious matters were still affairs of state. The Faith of the king was the Faith of his subjects. This is why Henry VIII's personal marital difficulties were able to change the course of English history.

Henry was increasingly frustrated because his wife of over twenty years, Catherine of Aragon, had failed to bear him a healthy son and heir. She had conceived six times, it is true, and given birth to Prince Henry in 1511 (who only survived a few days) and Princess Mary five years later. But royal marriages were not confected out of love but out of the political necessity to provide for a stable succession; otherwise political crisis was likely. Let it not be forgotten that the Wars of the Roses were still within living memory and the Tudor dynasty only recently established, thanks to victory in battle at Bosworth Field (1485). A young prince and heir seemed an absolute necessity.

Henry's frustration coincided with doubts over the validity of his marriage, especially in the light of Leviticus 20:21, which said that if a man slept with his brother's wife they would be childless. Catherine had previously been married to Henry's older brother, Arthur, who died in 1502. But then, his critics argued, Deuteronomy 25:5 instructed a brother to marry his widowed sister-in-law, the passage in Leviticus being aimed at the sin of adultery, though Henry's supporters discounted the Deuteronomy passage as a Jewish custom rather than a divine law.

In Henry's mind, the simplest solution to his 'Great Matter' was to apply for an annulment from Rome. Indeed, the king of France had only recently had his marriage annulled, his former queen, St Jane of Valois, going on to establish an order of nuns. However, papal dispensation had been required for Henry's marriage to occur in the first place and theological opinion remained generally on the queen's side. After all, the lady Henry now wanted to marry, Anne Boleyn, was actually related to him to the same degree of consanguinity as Catherine because her sister had formerly been his mistress. The crisis dragged on and reached a stalemate. The Holy See was reluctant to compromise the sanctity of matrimony and its own power to issue dispensations; nor did it desire to displease Catherine's nephew, the Emperor Charles V, who sacked Rome in 1527 and held the Pope and his cardinals virtual prisoners.

Breach with Rome

Meanwhile Henry was played upon by those at court who sympathised with the Protestant reformers, especially after the fall of the all-powerful Cardinal Wolsey in 1529. These included Thomas Cromwell (the son of a Putney tavern-keeper, and Chief Minister from 1532), and Thomas Cranmer, a Cambridge theologian who was Archbishop of Canterbury from 1533. It was suggested that, according to ancient authorities, the king had *imperium* (supreme authority) over both Church and State in his realms. Gradually during the early 1530s legislation was introduced limiting papal authority in England, such as the Act in Restraint of Appeals (1533) which prevented appeals from being sent to Rome and can be seen a first step towards schism. The following year saw this severance from Rome solidify - the Pope could no longer make ecclesiastical appointments or receive annates (the first year's revenue of bishoprics), which were now paid to the Crown. Most seriously, the Act of Supremacy (1534) declared Henry as Supreme Head of the English Church and the Act Extinguishing the Authority of the Bishop of Rome (1535) prohibited the exercise or defence of papal authority in any form.

Henry, meanwhile, had married Anne Boleyn, Cranmer declaring his previous marriage invalid. As is well known, his new consort proved equally unsuccessful in producing a son and was promptly despatched by a headsman's sword; the long-for prince was only produced by wife number three, Jane Seymour, who died in childbirth. Henry's personal life took the appearance of an on-going tragedy.

By breaking communion with the Bishop of Rome, Henry effectively made himself into a 'national pope'. He never claimed sacramental orders but, with Cromwell as his vicegerent in spiritual affairs, clearly exercised authority not only over the workings of the Church but the consciences of his subjects. According to one historian, his legacy was "to uncover the power of the English crown"; under his rule "parliament did his will; the great of the land walked wary of him; [and] he laid the ghost of Thomas Becket".[4]

Henry is often described as a religious conservative. Despite his break with Rome, he continued to attend Mass daily and frowned upon such Protestant innovations as clerical marriage or justification by faith alone. The *Ten Articles* of 1536 affirmed belief in the Real Presence and the necessity of confession. Henry even passed the Act for the Advancement of True Religion (1543), restricting the reading of the Bible to clerics and those of higher birth or education. However, his religious policy was radical. Shrines were destroyed, statues and windows smashed, pilgrimages suppressed and monasteries dissolved. Religious houses had been forcibly closed before - St John Fisher had even dissolved two nunneries and used the revenues to support St John's College, Cambridge - but Henry's policy was something new. Attacked for their opposition to the divorce and their links to the Catholic world beyond the Channel, the monasteries also provided land and money which the Crown needed to fight war and win the support of the nobles. However, they left not only picturesque ruins that would haunt the popular imagination for centuries to come but a huge gap in the field of education, medical care and poor relief. The dispossessed monks and nuns were given pensions; some seemed quietly to continue their way of life behind closed doors.

Not surprisingly, there was opposition to these revolutionary changes. 1535 saw the execution of several prominent figures who had refused to support the King's Supremacy, most notably the Bishop of Rochester (St John Fisher), the former Lord Chancellor (St Thomas More) and three Carthusian priors. The following year there were risings in Lincolnshire, Yorkshire, Cumberland and elsewhere, known as the 'Pilgrimage of Grace', involving thousands of ordinary people. Although, as always, religious motives were mixed with politico-economic grievances, the rebels marched under the banner of the Five Precious Wounds and criticised the king's religious policy, especially the dissolution of the monasteries.

Another prominent defender of the old Faith was Reginald Pole, whose veins brimmed with Plantagenet blood and whose education had been sponsored by Henry. He managed to escape to the continent - wisely enough, for even his mother (Blessed Margaret Pole) became a victim of the king's aggression. Beyond the Channel he wrote of the king acting as "a wild beast" and was made a cardinal.

There had been critics of the medieval Church before the break with Rome - one of the most vocal was St Thomas More - but there was no widespread hostility to the traditional faith and no real desire to support Protestantism. Moreover, the English were used to battles between the Throne and the Altar. Things, surely, would one day sort themselves out, just as they had in the days of King John or Henry II.

After Henry

The path taken by the Reformation in England was complex, gradual and piecemeal and its success was by no means guaranteed. There was much uncertainty, as each of Henry's children pursued a very different policy. The reign of the boy king Edward VI saw the continued destruction of Catholic England and moved the Church of England in the direction of Calvinist Geneva. The *Books of Common Prayer* issued in 1549 and 1552, based on both the Roman Missal and German sources, marked a significant change. The Sacrifice of the Mass was replaced by a Communion Service; the Liturgy of the Hours was radically simplified;

the old vestiges of Latin disappeared; church images continued to be whitewashed or removed. Liturgical changes, then as now, tended to be emotive and when the old Latin Mass was at last suppressed at Pentecost 1549 and replaced by the new *Prayer Book*, there was a popular uprising in the West Country, the so-called 'Prayer Book Rebellion'. Motivations were not exclusively spiritual but there was much discontent with the changes 'from above', the parishioners of Sampford Courtenay (Devon) complaining that the new English liturgy was "but like a Christmas game." Several thousand lost their lives in the resulting conflict.

When Edward died in 1553, his sister Mary briefly restored England to Catholicism, with the help of Cardinal Pole, who returned to England as Archbishop of Canterbury and Papal Legate. On 30th November 1554 he reconciled the realm to the Holy See during an emotionally-charged service at Whitehall. "If the angels in Heaven," the cardinal said, "rejoice over the conversion of a single sinner, what must be their joy to-day at the sight of a whole kingdom which repenteth?"

The queen and the cardinal took a realistic approach to Catholic restoration, confirming property rights and slowly refounding some of the dissolved monasteries. However, it is interesting that shrines and chantries were not restored. Pole organised a Legatine Synod, which stressed the importance of the residence of clergy and of preaching and catechesis in each parish. Most notably, he decreed "that in Cathedrals a certain number of initiated persons be brought up, whence as from a Seminary, men may be chosen who may be worthily set over Churches." The cardinal was one of the first to speak of seminaries and thus anticipated the Tridentine decrees, though his vision would not be actualised on English soil for another two and a half centuries. More controversial were the burnings of over three hundred Protestants, including Thomas Cranmer. About a sixth of the victims were women. For subsequent generations of Protestant Englishmen who devoured John Foxe's hugely influential *Actes and Monuments* (known as *Foxe's Book of Martyrs*), they remained a stark warning of the perceived horrors of popish rule.

Mary and Pole both died, as it happens, on 17th November 1558, leaving behind a tantalising historical 'what if'. It has been suggested that, if Mary had lived even a decade longer, after her death there might have been "a union of England and Scotland under Mary Stuart, followed by a Catholic British Empire"; "the triumph of Protestantism in England, far from being either natural or inevitable, was the result of one woman's premature death."[5]

The Elizabethan Settlement

The reign of Elizabeth I was indeed crucial for our story. She reigned for forty-five years - a length of time that allowed things to stabilise. Hopes of a Catholic restoration were dashed as each year of the reign began and as each Catholic suitor for a royal marriage was brushed to one side. At first, the queen turned a half-blind eye to those who did not conform but the situation changed dramatically ten years into her reign. First, in 1568, Mary the deposed queen of Scots arrived in England as a 'guest' of the Queen. A Catholic and next in the line of succession, she became the focus of many plots over the next two decades. The first of these took place in 1569, when the Earls of Northumberland and Westmorland led a Catholic rebellion, known as the 'Northern Rising'. Needless to say it failed. The following year the Pope sent a Bull excommunicating Elizabeth, originally planned to coincide with the previous year's rebellion. An armed rising and a papal excommunication hardly endeared England's Catholics to the queen. 'Penal laws' were passed, subjecting Catholics to fines and other penalties for practising their faith and not attending the 'official' church. It was treasonable to call the queen a heretic and to bring papal bulls (or even devotional items) into the country. Moreover, in 1571 restrictions were place on those travelling to the continent.

Matters worsened throughout the 1570s. The St Bartholomew's Day Massacre in Paris (1572) alerted Protestants once again to the perceived dangers of Catholicism, while there were rumours of a papally-sponsored invasion of Ireland; a Surrey-born priest, Nicholas Sanders, actually landed at Smerwick (Kerry) in 1580 with six hundred Spanish and Italian troops but was soon defeated. A new injection of life was given to English Catholics by the arrival of the first missionary priests, trained at the seminaries overseas - the cause of much alarm, for the authorities had hoped that the old faith would simply die out, as it had done in parts of northern Europe. In 1568 one of the growing band of Catholic exiles, William Allen, founded an 'English College' at Douai, a town which was close to the Channel and the home of a recently-founded University. Allen's College provided new blood for the underground English Church in the form of 440 priests who worked on the Elizabethan Mission. A group of these exiles produced the *Douay-Rheims Bible* in English, which was later used as one of the sources by the translators of the *King James Version*. Douai became an important centre for British Catholic exiles, with not only an English but also an Irish and a Scots College, as well as houses for English Benedictines and Franciscans. In 1579 another English College was founded by Allen in Rome and this was followed by other colleges, monasteries and convents overseas.

It was, moreover, not only secular priests who started arriving on English shores but Jesuits, the shock-troops of the Catholic Reformation, led by the likes of St Edmund Campion and Fr Robert Persons - men of great learning and holiness. This led to further penal legislation, making it treasonable to reconcile anyone or be reconciled to 'the Romish religion' (1581) and treason simply to be a priest on English soil (a novel departure for there was no need to have actually committed a crime) and felony to harbour one (1585). The punishment for treason was hanging, drawing and quartering - a hideous penalty that was designed utterly to obliterate the victim from society and memory.

An Age of Martyrs

It has been estimated that five thousand people were executed in Europe for religious reasons during the Reformation period, mostly in the Low Countries, France and England. It is interesting that most of the Catholic martyrs of the period were produced by England and Wales. However, the persecution of Catholics in England remained sporadic, flaring up at times of national crisis (for example, the aftermath of the Spanish Armada) and dying down in times of peace. Catholicism survived not only because of the heroism of the few but because many local officials were reluctant to take action against their popish neighbours. It may not have been the most intensive of persecutions, compared to some of those of the twentieth century, but the penal legislation remained on the statute books for several centuries.

The Martyrs became a vital part of the identity of English Catholicism, even for their contemporaries. At the English College in Rome gruesome paintings of the great martyrs of the past and present were commissioned to inspire the young seminarians, while a missionary oath was drawn up, by which students swore their "abiding readiness to return to England there to preach Catholic doctrine in face of all dangers." The names of those who took this oath were inscribed in what became known as the *Liber ruber* (the red book), sanctified by the blood of the martyrs, starting with St Ralph Sherwin in 1581. The College soon became known as 'the seminary of the martyrs' and St Philip Neri, who lived opposite the College for a time, used to greet students with the words *Salvete flores martyrum* (Hail! Flower of the Martyrs).

Many are the stories that have come down to us about the supreme act of witness of these martyrs, who suffered between 1535 and 1680. Blessed John Sandys was allowed to celebrate Mass the morning of his execution and delivered a moving exhortation to the congregation; Blessed Alexander Crowe freshly shaved a tonsure on his head to show his pride in the priesthood on the day of his death; Blessed Richard Simpson embraced the ladder and kissed its steps as he was led to the gallows. Blessed Nicholas Postgate welcomed his execution "as a short cut to heaven", while Blessed Joseph Lambton encouraged his fellow victims with the words, "Let us be merry, for tomorrow I hope we shall have a heavenly breakfast." Perhaps most memorably, when Blessed Roger Wrenno was hanged for harbouring a priest in 1616, the rope snapped and he was offered his life if only he took the Oath of Allegiance. It must have been a tempting offer, given the pains that he had briefly experienced at the end of the rope. But instead he rushed back up the ladder, saying he was the same man as before and that he had been granted a glimpse of heaven to which he now wanted to return.

Compromise and Survival

Despite the modest number of English Catholics in proportion to the general population, the idea and threat of Catholicism would dominate the national psyche for centuries. Indeed, the fierce nature of the persecutions reflected the insecurity of the Protestant nation. As new plots and conspiracies were uncovered, Catholics came to be tarred with the same brush and questions were raised about how one could be a good Catholic and a loyal Englishman at the same time.

Anti-Catholicism became part of the English identity. This can be seen at work in the way we traditionally view history - Elizabeth was 'Good Queen Bess', 'Gloriana', while her Catholic sister was 'Bloody Mary'. The Jesuits in particular became the bogey-men of the popular imagination, with their allegedly corrupt ways, their secretive plots and their Fifth Columnist tendencies.

From the succession of Elizabeth onwards the English Catholic Church took on a new identity that would last for the best part of three centuries. It would be a minority, underground Church. Some lived a sort of double life, attending the local Anglican church in order to avoid the fines but also receiving the Catholic sacraments. These were called 'Church Papists'. Then there were the out-and-out recusants, who separated themselves from the local parish (a radical step for the parish was not just a religious unit but very much at the heart of the local community) and regarded the 'Church Papists' with suspicion. Sometimes it was heads of households that occasionally conformed while the women and younger children stayed at home as recusants. Such was the nature of the times, that there were different levels of conformity and compromise.

The survival of Catholicism was largely due to those who made their homes strongholds of the old faith. Priests would come and go, arriving in disguise and with a confusing set of aliases; sometimes they were employed as a steward or tutor; when necessary, they made use of the hiding holes that were ingeniously designed by craftsmen such as St Nicholas Owen. Much depended on Catholic women to make the relevant domestic arrangements and pass the Faith on to the next generation. St Margaret Clitherow, for example, who was pressed to death in 1586, ran a school at her home in York's Shambles and sheltered priests, even though she was virtually a neighbour of the strongly Protestant Earl of Huntingdon, President of the Council of the North.

An ongoing problem was that of pastoral leadership. There was, firstly, an increasingly 'seigneurial' dimension, with the Catholic aristocracy and gentry beginning to see themselves as the effective employers, even 'superiors' of the clergy. This was little surprise given the lack of diocesan bishops. From 1581 William Allen (cardinal from 1587) acted as Prefect of the English Mission, with an unofficial jurisdiction over the secular clergy. The last of the Marian bishops, Thomas Goldwell of St Asaph's, died in 1585. He had joined the Theatines (one of the new orders of the 'Counter Reformation'), acted for a time as St Charles Borromeo's Vicar General in Milan and was the only English bishop to attend the Council of Trent.[6]

Cardinal Allen died in 1594 and four years later George Blackwell was appointed as Archpriest, a new office which gave him authority over the secular clergy of England and Scotland, with the help of twelve assistants. Almost immediately there was controversy for he was considered too 'pro-Jesuit'. This was one of the chief fault lines within the English Catholic community during the period. Broadly speaking, the Jesuits saw England as missionary territory, in need of a fresh start and new methodology. The seculars had a less radical vision, stressing the continuities with the pre-Reformation Church and seeing the Elizabethan regime as a blip. Many of the seculars appealed to Rome over Blackwell, gaining them the name of 'Appellants', and even drafted a 'Protestation of Allegiance' to the queen in the last year of her life. Despite all the imprisonments and executions of recent decades, there still seemed the chance of accommodation with the State in return for certain guarantees.

Catholicism under the Stuarts

The accession in 1603 of James I, son of Mary Stuart, raised Catholic expectations. That many of these hopes were soon dashed is apparent from the Gunpowder Plot of 1605, when a small group of Catholics, including Guy Fawkes, nearly succeeded in blowing up Parliament. Yet conditions for Catholics generally improved under James I and Charles I. Between 1618 and 1641 there were only two martyrdoms and from 1634 a succession of papal agents resided in London.

A further promising development was the possibility of setting up a colony in the New World, where Catholics and Protestants might live together in relative harmony. This was not an option open to many but it was chosen by the wealthy Calvert family from Yorkshire, who were granted land in the Chesapeake Bay area by Charles I in 1632. The new colony was named 'Maryland' (*Terra Mariae*), after Charles I's queen, the Catholic Henrietta Maria, and based upon the radical principles of liberty of conscience and the lack of an established religion. The English Jesuits were closely involved in the early years of the colony and built a Catholic church in St Mary's City - something which would have been impossible in England. Fr Andrew White, the London-born 'Apostle of Maryland', even composed books in the local Algonquian dialect and baptised a Indian chief, who took the name 'Charles'. The Calverts were overthrown in 1688 but a century or so later Maryland became the seat of the first American Catholic diocese.

In London Catholicism was flaunted semi-publicly in the foreign embassies and at Court. The Stuarts, up until 1688, had Catholic consorts - princesses from Catholic countries (Henrietta Maria, Catherine of Braganza and Mary of Modena) or converts to the Faith (Anne of Denmark). Catholic queens demanded Catholic chaplains; Henrietta Maria initially had a French bishop and twenty-seven priests in her household. One of the chaplains of Mary of Modena, when she was Duchess of York, was the Jesuit St Claude de la Colombière. Before coming to England he had been spiritual director to St Margaret Mary. Protestant London therefore became one of the first places to where the 'new' devotion to the Sacred Heart of Jesus was proclaimed.

Charles I's perceived Catholic tendencies and his support of the 'High Church' Archbishop Laud was one of the sparks that led to the Civil Wars. After the long years of the Personal Rule (1629-40), when the king did not call Parliament, the persecution of Catholics resumed in 1641. Interestingly, under the Protectorate of Oliver Cromwell (1653-58), only one priest was executed: St

John Southworth (1654), but even then he was put to death under a previous conviction (1627) which had been commuted to perpetual banishment provided he never returned to England.

The Restoration of Charles II in 1660 once again led to high hopes. The king had partly owed his escape after the Battle of Worcester (1651) to the assistance of Catholics and during his nine years of exile had frequent contact with the Catholic diaspora. On his deathbed in 1685, it became clear where his heart truly lay and he was reconciled to the Church. However his reign had seen an extension rather than an end to the penal laws. In 1673, for example, the Test Act introduced oaths of supremacy and allegiance and a declaration against transubstantiation for holders of public office. After the fictitious Popish Plot of 1678, dreamt up by an ex-seminarian called Titus Oates, there was a final crop of martyrs, including St Oliver Plunkett, Archbishop of Armagh and Primate of All Ireland (1681).

With the accession of Charles's Catholic brother, James II, it seemed that things could indeed change for the better. He was enough of a pragmatist to be crowned according to Anglican rites and quickly summoned Parliaments in England and Scotland, which assured him of their loyalty. By 1688, however, the situation was very different, thanks to the combination of the unexpected birth of a (Catholic) son and heir; the calculating opportunism of his Dutch Calvinist son-in-law, William of Orange; and the misinterpretation of many of his policies. His vision, indeed, was a progressive one - liberty of conscience and freedom of worship. As Duke of York, he had even promoted toleration towards the Jews in his private colony of New York. Sadly, England was not ready for his grand designs and the king's Catholicism meant that his policies were given the most sinister of interpretations. Thus, religious toleration was perceived to threaten the position of the Church of England and serve as a sly means of re-Catholicism. By the end of 1688 James found himself in exile at Saint-Germain-en-Laye, near Paris.

James II, however, could be said to have laid the foundations of the modern English Catholic Church. Throughout the seventeenth century, there were several attempts at solving the problem of Church leadership. After the Archpriests, came the appointment of a Vicar Apostolic of England - in episcopal orders but directly subject to Rome - and a period of governance by a Chapter of secular clergy. Under James, the former system was reintroduced. In 1685 John Leyburn, formerly President of the English College, Douai, was appointed as Vicar Apostolic of England. It was the first time a Catholic bishop had been present in England for nearly sixty years and he made a countrywide visitation to administer Confirmation. In his tour of the north in 1687 some 20,859 Catholics received the sacrament. The following year the English Catholic Church was split up into four Districts

(London, Midland, Northern and Western), each with its own Vicar Apostolic, and this system remained in place until the mid-nineteenth century. Soon afterwards they signed a joint Pastoral proclaiming the beginning of a new era. If the Faith had previously been a necessarily private and discreet affair, the bishops wrote, "now you are in Circumstances of letting it appear abroad, and of edifying your Neighbours by professing it publicly, and living up to the Rules prescribed by it".

The "Second Spring" and its aftermath

Persecution (at least of a physical kind) died down in the eighteenth century, although Catholics were suspected (often correctly) of not fully supporting the Protestant Hanoverian monarchy and backing the various Jacobite rebellions, which tried to put a Catholic Stuart back on the throne. The papacy supported the cause of the exiled James II and his son, 'James III', giving the latter a palace in Rome and his younger son, Henry Benedict, a cardinal's hat (he was known as the 'Cardinal Duke of York'). It was only in 1766 that the Holy See recognised the Hanoverian king of Great Britain.

The eighteenth century is often seen as one of malaise but there were some key developments: the centre of gravity for English Catholicism gradually moved from the lay patron (normally a member of the Catholic aristocracy or gentry) to the bishops (whose authority was consolidated), and from remote rural missions to the growing towns.

But life could still be difficult. Members of the clergy were periodically charged for "exercising the function of a popish priest" and had to be discreet. When Dom Thomas Benedict Shuttleworth began celebrating Mass at Warrington (Cheshire) in 1755, he travelled dressed as

Queen Elizabeth II and Prince Philip talk with Pope Benedict XVI during an audience at the Palace of Holyrood House in Edinburgh during the historic Papal Visit of 2010.

a packman and advertised his presence by a boy singing 'Sally in the Alley'.

The most famous Catholic leader of the eighteenth century, the saintly Richard Challoner, Vicar Apostolic of the London District, still had to be disguised as a layman and celebrate Mass discreetly in London pubs and cockpits. Despite his own poverty, he managed to establish schools and wrote a whole library of books for English Catholics - devotional works like *The Garden of the Soul* and *Meditations for Every Day of the Year*, historical volumes such as *The Memoirs of the Missionary Priests* (an important source book for the English Martyrs), not to mention a revision of the *Douay-Rheims Bible*. Challoner even had nominal responsibility for the Catholics in the British Colonies, including much of North America and the West Indies.

A further burden was added by Hardwick's Marriage Act (1753), which exempted only Jews and Quakers from the demand that all weddings should be celebrated before an Anglican clergyman. Although intended to address the problem of clandestine marriages, this necessitated two ceremonies for Catholics - one in front of the Anglican pastor and one before their own priest. This remained the case until the Registration Act of 1836.

The end of the eighteenth century saw many challenges to the old order - the ideas of the 'Enlightenment', the American War of Independence and, most notably, the

French Revolution, with its purge of monarchy, aristocracy and clergy. Old differences dating from the Reformation suddenly seemed less important as the ruling classes united to oppose the new common enemy - political radicalism and revolution. This can be seen in the way England welcomed five and a half thousand French clergy in the 1790s - seen as brave refugees rather than sinister, 'popish' priests (though anti-Catholicism was never far away). Some founded chapels which would later blossom into parishes. Many of the institutions founded overseas in exile now returned home, ironically finding Protestant Britain more secure than Catholic Europe. The English College of Douai continued at St Edmund's, Old Hall Green (Hertfordshire) and St Cuthbert's, Ushaw (County Durham). The Benedictine houses of Douai and Dieulouard transferred to Downside (Somerset) and Ampleforth (Yorkshire), while the former Jesuits set up a school at Stonyhurst (Lancashire), descended from the college at St Omer.

Catholic Relief and Emancipation

The bonding together of traditional forces and new ideas of civil liberty and tolerance led to changes in the law. A series of Relief Acts, starting in the 1770s, made life easier for English Catholics. The Act of 1778 allowed Catholics to join the Army and own and inherit property. It also abolished the £100 reward for those who informed against Catholic priests and schoolmasters. Despite its limited nature, there was much opposition. John Wesley, the founder of Methodism, wrote of the "purple power of Rome advancing by hasty strides to overspread this once happy nation." In June 1780 in another response to the Relief Act, the most serious English riots of the century broke out, led by Lord George Gordon - 285 lost their lives and several Catholic churches were badly damaged.

The Relief Act of 1791 permitted Catholic worship in registered churches, provided they had no bell or steeple, and allowed the establishment of schools. The Catholic cause was given a further boost by the union of Great Britain and Ireland in 1800-1. This brought Irish - and therefore Catholic - questions to the fore in Westminster. Indeed, it was 'the Liberator' himself, Daniel O'Connell, who became an energetic supporter of a further piece of legislation, the Catholic Emancipation Act. Lifting further restrictions and allowing Catholics to enter Parliament, he saw this as a vital step towards his aim of Home Rule for Ireland. The Act passed in 1829, thanks largely to the support of the Duke of Wellington (Prime Minister). There was much opposition and when the Earl of Winchilsea accused Wellington of working "for the infringement of our liberties and the introduction of Popery into every department of State," the Prime Minister challenged him to a duel on Battersea Fields.

The Relief Acts were, in part, the result of negotiations made by the Catholic Committee, a group of prominent laymen, but some of their proposals created controversy - such as the exact wording of the oath that was to be taken by Catholics in public office, the suggestion that the Government should have a veto over episcopal appointments or the hotly-debated *Exequatur*, giving the Crown the right to approve Roman documents. Similar measures could be found in many Catholic countries. John Milner, who became Vicar Apostolic of the Midland District in 1803, was particularly vigilant in making sure the Church's authority was not compromised and keeping in check "that system of lay interference and domination in the ecclesiastical affairs of English Catholics which has perpetuated divisions and irreligion among too many of them." Indeed, the period saw the gradual 'emancipation' not only of Catholics from penal legislation but of the clergy from lay dominance.

English Catholics were still a tiny minority but this was soon to change thanks to two factors. First, there was massive Irish immigration to England, especially in the aftermath of the 'Great Famine'. The Catholic population rocketed from less than 100,000 in 1800 to 750,000 in 1850. The numerical boom created a need for churches and schools, although this led to the impression that the Catholic community was an Irish ghetto, confirming the perception that Catholicism was somehow 'foreign' to England.

Another key factor was the Catholicising movement within the Church of England, led by Oxford scholars such as John Keble, Edward Bouverie Pusey and Blessed John Henry Newman. They rediscovered the 'Catholic' roots of the Church and looked to the early Church Fathers and the medieval centuries for inspiration. This headed in two directions - those who stayed within the Church of England (the 'Anglo-Catholic' or 'High Church' Anglicans) and those who 'crossed the Tiber' to Rome. There were many high profile converts, such as Newman (still remembered as the leading English theologian of modern times) and Henry Edward Manning (who became Archbishop of Westminster in 1865) among the clergy and, from the laity, the Marquis of Ripon (later Viceroy of India) and the Marquis of Bute (the richest man in Britain). Without the energy and financial support of many of these converts, English Catholicism would have developed differently and would have lacked many of its beautiful church buildings.

The expansion of the Church was further facilitated by the growth of the religious orders, building upon those who had already returned home after the French Revolution. The convert Ambrose Phillipps de Lisle presided over a Catholic revival around his estates in Leicestershire by supporting the foundation of the Cistercian abbey at Mount St Bernard's (1837) and inviting the Rosminian missionary, Fr Luigi Gentili, to preach in the surrounding villages. Another Italian order, the Passionists, did much work in the Midlands. It was one of its members, Blessed

Dominic Barberi, who in 1845 received Dr Newman into the Church - a 'secession' which rocked the Anglican establishment and led to many conversions. Shortly afterwards Newman, with the help of Frederick Faber, introduced the Oratory of St Philip Neri to England. Meanwhile, religious congregations for women were also opening convents and doing much in the field of education and medical care. These included several 'home grown' communities, such as Margaret Hallahan's Dominican Sisters at Coventry (1845) and Stone (1853).

The Restoration of the Hierarchy

In 1840 Pope Gregory XVI increased the number of Vicars Apostolic from four to eight. It was a sign of things to come. On 29th September 1850, Blessed Pius IX decreed that "the Hierarchy of Bishops Ordinary, taking their titles from their Sees, should, according to the usual rules of the Church, again flourish in the Kingdom of England." Initially there was one Province divided into twelve dioceses, headed by the Archbishop of Westminster - a title which in itself must have alarmed the British Establishment, for Westminster was at the very heart of the nation and its historic Abbey fell directly under the Crown. *The Times* complained that this 'papal aggression' was "one of the grossest acts of folly and impertinence which the Court of Rome has ventured to commit since the Crown and people of England threw off its yoke."

Matters were not helped by the emotional Pastoral Letter, 'From Without the Flaminian Gate', written by the new Cardinal Archbishop of Westminster, Nicholas Wiseman. He proclaimed that, by Papal Brief, "we govern and shall continue to govern, the counties of Middlesex, Hertford and Essex, as Ordinary thereof, and those of Surrey, Sussex, Kent, Berkshire, and Hampshire, with the islands annexed, as Administrator with Ordinary jurisdiction". This caused uproar - Queen Victoria, perhaps understandably, asked: "Am I Queen of England or am I not?" and Lord Winchilsea even urged the declaration of war on the Papal States. It led to the sensational conversion of the Duke of Norfolk to Anglicanism and the Ecclesiastical Titles Act of 1851, prohibiting the Catholic assumption of Anglican episcopal titles, although Wiseman's hastily-written *Appeal to the Reason and Good Feeling of the English People* did something to defuse the situation.

The fifteen years of Wiseman's archiepiscopate were marred by internal disputes, caused in part by the mistrust of some of the 'old' English Catholics for the Cardinal's obvious penchant for converts, Italianate devotions and 'foreign' religious orders. The foundation of the Oblates of St Charles, a community of secular priests directly subject to the Archbishop and based on a similar Milanese community, led to the so-called 'Wars of Westminster' that pitted Wiseman and Fr Manning (the Provost) against Archbishop Errington (the Coadjutor) and much of the Chapter. However, despite his sometimes autocratic manner, Wiseman did much to build up the modern English Church. With a restored hierarchy and growing numbers, Catholics found a new self-confidence and became increasingly visible. This can be seen in the churches that were built - London, for instance, boasted 24 churches in 1826 and 102 in 1863. Many of these edifices were designed in the Gothic style, stressing continuity with the medieval past. The convert architect Augustus Welby Northmore Pugin in particular saw Gothic architecture (or his personal fusion of medieval styles) as the embodiment of Catholic England - designed for the proper worship of God, using local materials and springing from the principles of truth, goodness and beauty.

Priests were now known as 'Father' rather than 'Mr' and wore the Italian soutane (cassock) and biretta. Only a few decades previously William Poynter, Vicar Apostolic of the London District, had tended to wear brown suits when away from the sanctuary and was heard to remark on one occasion 'Church dress for Church use, sir.' English Catholics became used to a whole panoply of devotions, such as Corpus Christi processions, May Crownings, novenas and *Quarant' Ore*, all of which would have been unheard of in penal times, when piety tended to be undemonstrative and chapels were relatively unadorned. The religiosity of the people was stirred not only by recourse to the sacraments but the many lay associations (such as the Society of St Vincent de Paul), house-to-house visits and the occasional parish mission. The Church had indeed emerged from her recusant shell.

Education remained a high priority and the building of schools demanded much sacrifice. It was a case of 'Schools before Churches'. Cardinal Manning famously refused to push forward plans to build a Cathedral at Westminster till every Catholic child was placed in a Catholic school. Up until 1870 education had depended on initiatives by religious and philanthropic bodies, as well as private individuals. Even in penal times there were educational establishments scattered around the country, including convent schools at Hammersmith and York (Bar Convent). These were legally recognised in 1791 and in 1847 the Catholic Poor School Committee was founded to co-ordinate the Church's work and negotiate for government grants. The Forster Education Act of 1870 was the first major intervention by the government, setting up a dual system of State schools and those run by 'voluntary bodies'. No state funding was given to the voluntary sector, beyond minimal grants, and so Catholic schools relied on fees and collections to survive. It was estimated that up until 1902 Catholic expenditure on building schools was around £4 million, of which only £60,000 had come from the public purse.

Manning was also actively concerned with social affairs - as can be seen in his promotion of the temperance movement and his intervention in the London Dockers' Strike of 1889, which made him a hero to the working class. Some have identified his influence behind Leo XIII's epoch-making encyclical on the Church's social teaching, *Rerum Novarum* (1891); whatever the truth, the English cardinal certainly lived according to it.

By the end of the nineteenth century the Church had come a long way but emancipation for Catholics, in its broadest sense, was not yet complete. As one historian has noted:

> ...their churches could not have steeples; their priests could not wear clerical garb in public; their schools were denied state funding; they could not leave charitable bequests for purposes judged "superstitious" by Protestant standards. Roman Catholics also faced social discrimination. They were physically shunned; and the mass media of the day produced a torrent of tracts, books, magazines, and newspaper stories that reviled their beliefs, challenged their political loyalty, and depicted them as the deluded dupes of men who lusted for sex, money and power.[7]

The Hierarchy themselves imposed restrictions. It was not until 1895, for example, that permission was given for Catholics to enter Oxford and Cambridge. Manning, himself a Balliol man, had remained convinced that the non-Catholic environment of the Universities could easily corrupt souls and established a Catholic University College in Kensington, which eventually closed due to financial and administrative difficulties.

The Twentieth Century

The first half of the twentieth century saw the revived English Church come of age. It has been called "an era of steady expansion largely untroubled by internal dissent,"[8] though the modernist crisis at the turn of the century led to much intellectual turmoil and the suspension of a prominent Jesuit theologian, Fr George Tyrell. In 1903 Westminster Cathedral was finally completed and the first service to be held there was the Requiem of its builder, Herbert Cardinal Vaughan. Five years later, the papal constitution *Sapienti Consilio* removed Great Britain (along with the United States, Canada, Luxemburg and Holland) from the jurisdiction of the congregation Propaganda Fide, meaning they were no longer considered missionary territory. The same year, 1908, the International Eucharistic Congress was held in London and, for the first time since the reign of Mary I, a papal legate landed on English soil. Although the proposed Eucharistic procession through the streets of Westminster caused much controversy and had to be adapted, the Congress was a sign of the Church's new-found maturity. Also in 1908 Edward VII, Queen Alexandra and the Prince of Wales attended a Requiem for the assassinated king of Portugal at St James's Spanish Place in London - the first British monarch publicly to attend Mass since James II.

The Great War saw an enormous effort on the home front to help the soldiers in the theatres of war, including the disproportionate number of Irish Catholic troops. For many the war provided a first experience of Catholicism - the quiet piety of the Belgian and French civilians, the churches that stood in the zone of conflict, iconic images such as the leaning Virgin on the top of the church at Albert (it had been hit by Germans shells and was the subject of much mythology) and the dedication of the Catholic chaplains. The war resulted in many conversions.

As the Church grew, it was re-organised. In 1911 Liverpool and Birmingham became archiepiscopal sees, to be joined five years later by Cardiff. The Archbishop of Westminster was no longer the only Metropolitan in the country, though it was decreed that he should be the *Praeses Perpetuus* (Perpetual President) of the Hierarchy, chairing the meetings of bishops. The attitude of the government was also softening, for in 1915 a British Legation was established at the Vatican, aware of the important diplomatic role of the Catholic Church. Full relations were set up only in 1982. Another change occurred within a week of the 1918 Armistice: thanks to the new *Code of Canon Law*, pre-existing 'Missions' became fully-fledged 'Parishes'.

Meanwhile, in the field of education, there were vital developments. The 1902 Act set up local education authorities and allowed for the support of voluntary schools from the local rates in addition to government grants. For Catholics it meant that their schools were at last part of the national system and that vital help was given in funding teacher salaries and other running costs. Many outside the Church objected to the fact that taxpayers' money was used to fund Catholic education; 'Rome on the Rates'. With the election of a Liberal Government in 1906, there were fears that the Act might be repealed and the voluntary sector suppressed. Cardinal Bourne even organised a rally at the Albert Hall and worked hard to defeat three Bills that threatened Catholic interests. The 1944 Education Act, which promised 'secondary education for all', was a further important stage and designated Catholic schools as 'voluntary-aided'.

Writing in the mid-1930s, Fr David Mathew (later to become a bishop) summed up the English Catholicism of this period:

Altogether it was a strong-rooted Catholic life; the churches crowded for the Lenten Mission; the old men and women with their rosaries; the sometimes too-ordered crowds of school children; the collectors and the scrubbed and tousled altar boys. On the Sunday afternoons there were the Brothers of St Vincent de Paul upon their rounds; the tea on the hob and often the *News of the World* spread on the kitchen table; the mothers with the *Catholic Fireside* and the eldest daughter getting the children ready for Benediction. It was perhaps at the parochial gatherings that the spirit of those days was best caught up; the young men crowding at the back of the hall against the worn distemper; the parish clergy on the platform and, in so many cases, that memory of an Irish past, *Oh! Danny Boy*.[9]

The Archbishop of Westminster from 1935, Arthur Hinsley, was an untypical prelate. Having spent much of his life as a popular seminary rector in Rome and papal representative in British Africa, he was plucked out of retirement at a time of fast social change and the growing threat of totalitarianism overseas, especially in its Soviet and Nazi forms. Hinsley became an international voice promoting liberty and justice - something that would not have been possible even half a century earlier. As early as 1938 he was speaking at the Albert Hall against the Nazi persecution of the Jews, claiming that the Emperor Nero was "a model of justice compared to the Führer of the German Reich." As Hinsley was dying in 1943, his final public statement was produced for the World Jewish Congress in New York: "I denounce with utmost vigour the persecution of the Jews by the Nazi oppressors." German propaganda rightly called him a "friend of the Jewish people." He also showed sympathy towards the Catholics living under the Third Reich, who, along with "the members of the Evangelical Confessional Church, have been among the principal victims of the Nazi regime."

Those who so readily criticise the seeming 'silence' of Pius XII should remember the witness of local leaders such as Cardinal Hinsley.

English Catholicism received a great deal of prestige from many of its converts, including such literary luminaries as Ronald Knox, G. K. Chesterton and Evelyn Waugh. The period also saw rapid Catholic *embourgeoisement*; the faithful were just as likely to be white- as blue-collar workers. Even in the years following the Second World War, the Church seemed confident and stable; few expected the religious revolution that was just around the corner. New parishes continued to be set up; Wembley Stadium was filled for the celebrations of the Centenary of the Restoration of the Hierarchy (1950), for Fr Peyton's Rosary Crusade (1952) and for the Coronation of Our Lady of Willesden (1954). A Vocations Exhibition at Earl's Court as late as 1965 included a mass ordination of priests.

Epilogue

Into the Third Millennium

In 1962 St John XXIII opened the Second Vatican Council. It became the biggest global meeting of bishops in the Church's history, opening the windows of the Church and setting the priorities for believers in the modern age. Councils take time to be put into effect and initially there was confusion and disappointment at both ends of the spectrum. The Council coincided with the 1960s, which saw a social and sexual revolution, and a tendency to reject anything that seemed 'old-fashioned'. Some thought the Council did not go far enough. Many priests left active ministry, including the prominent theologian Fr Charles Davis (a *peritus* at the Council), and there was much dissent in the wake of *Humanae Vitae* (1968), which confirmed the Church's traditional teaching on artificial contraception. On the other side, many felt saddened at the disappearance of old certainties and at aspects of the liturgical reforms. The process of change was not always handled with sensitivity and, in some places, the proverbial baby was thrown out with the bathwater, as Catholic practice and catechesis were diluted to appear more 'relevant'. The bishops, with first William Cardinal

Godfrey and then John Carmel Cardinal Heenan at the forefront, tried their best to steer the Church during these turbulent times.

Today Catholics are still a minority but have become more and more a respected part of the nation. Cardinal Hume was widely respected as a spiritual leader and was awarded the Order of Merit by the Queen shortly before his death in 1999. When St John Paul II visited the UK in 1982, and his successor Benedict XVI in 2010, the whole country's gaze was on them. Recent decades have seen major new developments in the story of English Catholicism. On the one hand, many of the institutions of the "Second Spring" have been rationalised - parishes merged and churches, seminaries and convents closed. The terrible scourge of child abuse at the hands of priests and religious has caused much scandal and hurt. Added to this are huge changes in society and culture. The biggest challenge is no longer considered to be "our separated brethren", as it was a century ago, but religious indifference and aggressive atheism. The power of the media has used its resources in questioning and criticising the Church. Marriage has been redefined and laws passed which attack the very sanctity of life and the dignity of the human person.

There are also signs of growth. In many urban parishes there is an increasing Mass attendance, thanks largely to the presence of Catholic immigrants, who often bring with them a deep faith - showing that those from overseas continue to enrich the English Catholic community. There is a renewed interest in Scripture and Eucharistic adoration; new 'movements', such as Opus Dei, the Neo-Catechumenal Way or the Faith Movement, have brought new life to the Church, and there have been positive developments in catechesis and youth ministry (inspired by gatherings like World Youth Day). Catholics have also benefitted from the greater understanding and co-operation between Christians of different denominations, especially on the local level.

Benedict XVI's concern for the Sacred Liturgy has led to a deepened understanding of the *ars celebrandi*, a new English translation of the *Roman Missal* and the recognition of the 'extraordinary form' as an honoured part of the Roman Rite. Clergy numbers have been boosted by several waves of former clergymen from the Church of England (some of them married), most recently through the Personal Ordinariate of Our Lady of Walsingham. This was set up by the apostolic constitution *Anglicanorum coetibus* (2011) as a response to the groups of Anglicans who had "repeatedly and insistently" petitioned "to be received into full Catholic communion individually as well as corporately", while allowing them to retain some of their heritage and traditions. With this in mind, an Ordinariate Use was approved which drew liturgical texts from both the *Roman Missal* and the 1662 *Book of Common Prayer*. According to Pope Benedict, the Ordinariate helped "set our sights on the ultimate goal of all ecumenical activity: the restoration of full ecclesial communion in the context of which the mutual exchange of gifts from our respective spiritual patrimonies serves as an enrichment to us all."

There is a renewed involvement of the laity in the work of the Church, especially through pastoral and liturgical ministries and faith formation, although, as Pope Francis has noted, "this involvement is not reflected in a greater penetration of Christian values in the social, political and economic sectors. It often remains tied to tasks within the Church, without a real commitment to applying the Gospel to the transformation of society."[10]

* * * *

Every detail of the past shows the presence of Jesus Christ, who is the Lord of History. He was present in those who brought the Gospel to England and in the country's many saints. He was present in the sufferings of the martyrs and the quiet perseverance of the recusants. He was present in the lives of those who built our parishes and schools, the servants of the Second Spring.

Now he is present in us. We are links in this great chain of Faith. Let us pray that we will be faithful and courageous as we write the next chapter of this story.

Some Key Players in the History
of English Catholicism

St Alban (d. c.209), Proto-martyr of England

St Patrick (c.390-c.461), Apostle of Ireland

St Columba (c.521-597), monk, founder of Iona

St Gregory the Great (c.540-604),
Pope, 'Apostle of the English'

St Augustine of Canterbury (d. 604),
first Archbishop of Canterbury

St Paulinus (d. 644), first Bishop of York

St Æthelberht (560-616), first Christian King of Kent

St Edwin (d. 633), first Christian King of Northumbria

St Aidan (d. 651), Abbot-Bishop of Lindisfarne

St Cuthbert (d. 687), Abbot-Bishop of Lindisfarne

St Bede the Venerable (673-735),
historian, Doctor of the Church

St Boniface (680-754), Anglo-Saxon Apostle of Germany

St Hilda (614-680), Abbess of Whitby

Blessed Alcuin of York (c.735-804), scholar

St Dunstan (909-988), Archbishop of Canterbury

St Anselm (c.1033-1109), Archbishop of Canterbury, Doctor of the Church

St Thomas Becket (1118-70), Archbishop of Canterbury, martyr

Thomas Cardinal Wolsey (c.1470-1530), Archbishop of York, Lord Chancellor to Henry VIII

St John Fisher (1469-1535), Cardinal, Bishop of Rochester, martyr

St Thomas More (1478-1535), Lord Chancellor to Henry VIII, martyr

Reginald Cardinal Pole (1500-58), last Catholic Archbishop of Canterbury

William Cardinal Allen (1532-94), founder of the English Colleges at Douai and Rome, Prefect of the English Mission

St Edmund Campion (c.1540-81), Jesuit martyr

St Margaret Clitherow (1556-86), mother, wife and martyr of York

Bishop John Leyburn (1615-1702), Vicar Apostolic

Bishop Richard Challoner (1691-1781), Vicar Apostolic and writer

Fr Luigi Gentili (1801-48),
Rosminian missionary in England

Blessed Dominic Barberi (1792-1849),
Passionist missionary in England

Nicholas Cardinal Wiseman (1802-65),
first Archbishop of Westminster

Blessed John Henry Newman (1801-90), convert,
theologian, founder of the English Oratory

Henry Edward Cardinal Manning (1808-92), convert,
Archbishop of Westminster

Herbert Cardinal Vaughan (1832-1903),
Archbishop of Westminster

Arthur Cardinal Hinsley (1865-1943), Archbishop of
Westminster

Gilbert Keith Chesterton (1874-1936),
convert and journalist

Mgr Ronald Knox (1888-1957), convert priest
and writer

John Carmel Cardinal Heenan (1905-75), Archbishop
of Westminster

Basil Cardinal Hume (1923-99),
Archbishop of Westminster

Further Reading

J. C. H. Aveling *The Handle and the Axe*: *The Catholic Recusants in England from Reformation to Emancipation* (1976)

John Bossy *The English Catholic Community 1570-1850* (1979)

Michelle Brown *How Christianity Came to Britain and Ireland* (2005)

Eamon Duffy *The Stripping of the Altars*: *Traditional Religion in England 1400-1580* (2nd ed, 2005)

Eamon Duffy *The Voices of Morebath*: *Reformation and Rebellion in an English Village* (2003)

Gabriel Glickman *The English Catholic Communiy 1688-1745*: *Politics, Culture and Ideology* (2009)

V. Alan McClelland and Michael Hodgetts (eds.) *From Without the Flaminian Gate*: *150 Years of Roman Catholicism in England and Wales 1850-2000* (1999)

Edward Norman *The English Catholic Church in the Nineteenth Century* (1984)

Edward Norman *Roman Catholicism in England from the Elizabeth Settlement to the Second Vatican Council* (1985)

John Saward et al. (ed.) *Firmly I Believe and Truly*: *The Spiritual Tradition of Catholic England* (2011)

Nicholas Schofield and Gerard Skinner *The English Vicars Apostolic 1688-1850* (2009)

Barbara Yorke *The Conversion of Britain 600-800* (2006)

Endnotes

[1] Robin Fleming, *Britain After Rome: The Fall and the Rise 400-1070* (2011), p.61

[2] Michelle P. Brown, *How Christianity Came to Britain and Ireland* (2006), p.189

[3] Christopher Dawson, *Medieval Essays* (1953; rept. 2002), p.78

[4] Eric Ives, *Henry VIII* (2007) p.107

[5] Susan Doran & Thomas S. Freeman (ed.), *Mary Tudor: Old and New Perspectives* (2011), p.1

[6] Living in Rome for much of his later years, he ordained the Spanish composer Tomás Luis de Victoria as a priest.

[7] D. G. Paz, *Popular Anti-Catholicism in Mid-Victorian England* (1992) pp.1-2

[8] Sheridan Gilley 'The Years of Equipoise, 1892-1943', in V. Alan McClelland and Michael Hodgetts (eds.) *From Without the Flaminian Gate: 150 Years of Roman Catholicism in England and Wales 1850-2000* (1999), p.21

[9] David Mathew, *Catholicism in England 1535-1935* (1938), p. 246

[10] Pope Francis, *Evangelii Gaudium*, 102

Reformation in England

Dr Raymond Edwards

The events of the 'Reformation' led to centuries of bitter
theological disputes, wars, persecutions and power struggles
and its consequences endure to this day. This booklet looks
at the events which led up to the Reformation in Europe, and
particularly in England. It shows how much that was good was
lost in this conflict.

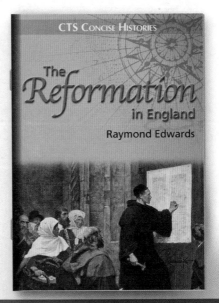

H505   ISBN 978 1 86082 385 5

The Early Church

Fr Anthony Meredith, SJ

The growth of the Church in her first three hundred years was faster and stronger than can easily be accounted for on purely historical grounds. While Christianity offered a brighter hope to a weary world than rival religions, it demanded a drastic change of life: the courage of Christians under persecution and their care for the poor and widows were remarkable, but in the end Fr. Meredith attributes her remarkable vigour to her message about Jesus and the continuous guidance of the Holy Spirit.

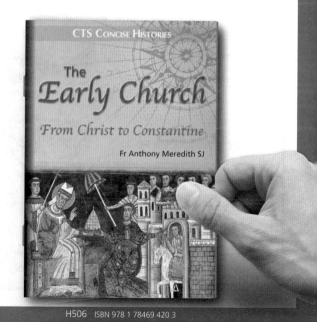

H506   ISBN 978 1 78469 420 3